A Beginners Guide To
Brazilian Jiu Jitsu

"Be so strong that nothing can disturb your peace of mind."

~Grand Master Carlos Gracie, First Commandment, *12 Commandments of Brazilian Jiu Jitsu*

Table of Contents

A Beginners Guide To Brazilian Jiu Jitsu............................ 1

Table of Contents... 3

What is Brazilian Jiu Jitsu? 4

What happens in a typical Brazilian Jiu Jitsu class?...................... 16

Some Basic Effective Techniques for BJJ 33

Competing in your first BJJ tournament......................... 48

Coming Back from an Injury.. 62

Why do so many students stop training? And how to stop it from being you.. 66

Beginning Judo: The Ultimate Guide to Starting Judo.................. 70

MMA: Beginning MMA: The Ultimate Guide to MMA Training... 72

People who are unfamiliar with the martial arts disciplines are often surprised to learn that Brazilian Jiu Jitsu is much more than a rigid system of programmed moves, throws, and strikes, and holds. No, if that were the case, it would be an extremely poor philosophy that would only have value in physical conflicts – and very limited value, at that.

No, Brazilian Jiu Jitsu transcends a mere fighting style – it is a martial art form that, when practiced correctly, becomes an actual way of life. The proper application of the philosophies, techniques, mindsets, and principles that Brazilian Jiu Jitsu teaches will help its student's live productive, balanced, healthy, and personally-fulfilling lives.

To demonstrate how this can be achieved, it might be best to attempt to answer some of the most-<u>Frequently Asked Questions</u> asked by people who are new to the sport.

What is Brazilian Jiu Jitsu?

Brazilian Jiu Jitsu, also commonly referred to as BJJ, is simultaneously –

- *a traditional "modern" martial art* – because it is a system that teaches a series of fighting techniques and practices that have been passed down from Grand Masters and other teachers to students for generations.

  What is now known as Brazilian Jiu Jitsu (early 20th-century) evolved from Judo (late 19th century), which itself was in evolution of earlier Japanese Jujutsu. Thus, BJJ's roots can be traced back as far as perhaps the late 1400's.

The name itself translates into "the gentle art/skill", because it utilizes the concepts of balance and leverage and balance, rather than force.

- _a self-defense system_ – because unlike many martial art forms, it emphasizes real-life situations and effective results, instead of regimented forms and flashy kicks and throws – the kind you might see during formal competitions showcasing other disciplines.

During instruction is not uncommon to learn practical techniques about how to handle such situations as escaping from headlocks or chokeholds that might be employed by street assailants, or how to deal with knife or gun attacks.

One of the primary lessons taught is that anyone can learn to defend themselves against an attacker – _quickly, effectively, and decisively_ – regardless of their size or strength.

Even the "legendary" names in BJJ demonstrated their philosophy of emphasizing substance – i.e., _results_ – over style.

"We don't believe in teaching a ton of moves every class, and the student walking away with limited knowledge. We prefer our students to know 20 techniques at 100%, rather than 100 techniques at 20%."

~ Royce Gracie, UFC Hall of Famer, considered perhaps the most influential person in the history of modern Mixed Martial Arts

- *a combat sport* – no other martial arts discipline has been as influential on the rise in popularity of modern-day Mixed Martial Arts. MMA combines striking techniques from other combat sports such as boxing and kickboxing, but surpasses them both with BJJ grappling techniques.

  Royce Gracie is the son of Helio Gracie, one of the originators of modern Brazilian Jiu Jitsu. As a mixed martial artist, Royce won UFC 1, UFC 2, UFC 4, and battle to a draw in the Championship Fight in UFC 5. He also holds the record for most consecutive submission victories – 11.

  Ronda Rousey is the current UFC Women's Bantamweight Champion. She is undefeated, primarily due to her skill in BJJ (as well as her Judo). Her preferred method is to take her opponent down to the ground – *a BJJ staple* – and end the fight quickly by submission by armbar. She holds the record for fastest submission in UFC championship history – 14 seconds.

- *a way of life* – because it encourages and teaches students to live healthy, contented, and balanced lives by applying the core principles of patience, control, and efficiency to all areas of life, not just self-defense.

To a true practitioner of BJJ, <u>patience</u> means to maximize your chances of success by waiting until the moment is right to make your best move.

To a true practitioner of BJJ, <u>control</u> means to govern your own internal struggles, impetuosity, and desires in order to take charge of whatever situation you are in.

To a true practitioner of BJJ, <u>efficiency</u> means achieving the maximum results with the least possible effort. It means working with to achieve your goals as quickly and as directly as possible.

Lastly, a true practitioner of BJJ believes that they should always strive towards having a strong body, mind, and spirit. Mastery in these three aspects of life is best represented by a triangle.

The triangle is chosen as a strong symbol, because whenever a person is well-rounded in these three areas, they will always have a strong base supporting them.

If Brazilian Jiu Jitsu came from Judo, and Judo came from Japanese Jujutsu, what is the difference?

The differences between the three related-yet-distinct martial arts disciplines can be likened to the difference between a new car, an older car, and an antique automobile. There are similarities, but the new car is much more advanced, efficient and powerful than the earlier models.

- Ancient Jujutsu training focused on "*kata*" – rigid, pre-determined movement sequences of defense and attack. While kata training is important, it is not realistic or practical in a real-world combat situation.

- Judo training emphasizes "*randori*" – unpredictable, non-cooperated sparring between opponents. This is considered superior to the earlier forms and more applicable to actual fighting scenarios.

- Brazilian Jiu Jitsu surpasses Judo because it adds further emphasis on groundwork and grappling to the throws and strikes found in Judo. Learning to take an opponent to the ground is a major reason why BJJ is considered a superior form of self-defense, because on the ground, most advantages of size or strength are negated.

   For example, a competitive Judo match can be won by a pin or a throw, but not by a submission hold. A Brazilian Jiu Jitsu match may – *and frequently does* – end by submission, because BJJ strongly emphasizes position and leverage during the confrontation. I

Why should I train in Brazilian Jiu Jitsu? I just want to learn self-defense, not be an MMA fighter like I see on TV.

Knowing <u>why</u> you want to train is an important question to ask yourself before commencing instruction in any martial art. The great thing about Brazilian Jiu Jitsu is that it gives you several different options, based upon your interests, inclination, and abilities.

IF... you want to learn an effective means of <u>self-defense</u>, then Brazilian Jiu Jitsu may be your best choice. Again, BJJ is designed to allow a smaller or weaker individual to effectively defend against an attack by a larger or more powerful foe.

BJJ emphasizes real-world combat situations, not flashy techniques that may look great in the movies but which have no real applicability in an actual fight.

In a real life-or-death confrontation where withdrawal or retreat is not possible, the safest course is to end the fight as fast, effectively, and decisively as possible, not to "wow" your attacker with a series of fancy kicks and poses. After all, a person intent on doing you harm is not going to wait while you get into your proper *kata* stance.

Brazilian Jiu Jitsu emphasizes techniques that can be learned in a relatively short amount of time. This means that a person who may not have been training in BJJ for very long can still possess enough practical knowledge to protect themselves and in the event of an unavoidable confrontation.

Again, because there is so much emphasis on position and leverage, even people of limited athleticism, small stature, or without great physical strength can still learn how to quickly defeat, disable, or disarm an attacker.

The effectiveness of Brazilian Jiu Jitsu as a means of self-defense is evidenced by its acceptance by the United States Army. The Army's Combatives Manual was re-written in 2002 to incorporate the techniques of BJJ, and today, similar instruction is found in almost any law enforcement agency.

IF... on the other hand, you want to take up Brazilian Jiu Jitsu in order to <u>get in better shape</u>, then you will soon realize a multitude of benefits –

- <u>BJJ will increase your endurance</u>. Although you can begin at any fitness level, over time, your endurance will increase because of the demands of the sport.

- <u>BJJ will increase your flexibility</u>. The grappling and groundwork will initially put your body in unfamiliar positions, but again, over time, you will acclimate and become more flexible.

- <u>BJJ will help you build muscle and gain strength</u>. Even without extra weight training, you will find that because sparring invariably involves grappling with another human being, you will tone your muscles and get a lot stronger.

- <u>BJJ will improve your aerobic ability</u>. When you are involved in a combat-oriented, non-cooperative martial arts sparring session, there is no "down time". Because of the effort you put in, it is a great workout, and it is very likely that you will shed a few unwanted pounds.

- <u>BJJ will reduce your stress</u>. Strenuous physical activity of any sort is a great way to "sweat out" the stress found elsewhere in your life. There is nothing like taking out your daily frustrations on your sparring partner – in a safe and controlled manner, of course.

IF... you have tried other martial arts or combat sports and you like the idea of learning Brazilian Jiu Jitsu as a means to compete in mixed martial arts contests, you will find no shortage of challenges.

Because of its proven success against other martial arts disciplines, many newcomers to mixed martial arts enter competitions having only trained in Brazilian Jiu Jitsu. BJJ is a continually-evolving martial arts form, so there are always new techniques, holds, and counters that can be learned and developed, so there is no chance of boredom or burnout.

IF... you are excited about the idea of competition, but would rather stay within the Jiu Jitsu discipline rather than facing off against practitioners of other martial arts, there are also multiple opportunities to do so.

Brazilian Jiu Jitsu competitions are held in several ways. For example, there are some tournaments held where the victor is determined only by submission – no referee decisions, no points, and no advantages.

For the competitive soul, Brazilian Jiu Jitsu offers challenges and opportunities that are virtually unrivaled in other martial arts or combat sports.

Finally, **IF...** you have been searching for a way to add positive structure and balance to your life, then the philosophy behind Brazilian Jiu Jitsu might be exactly what you need.

When Grand Master Carlos Gracie Sr. came up with is "*12 Commandments of Brazilian Jiu Jitsu*", the wisdom he imparted did not describe new striking or submission techniques. In fact, he avoided talking directly about combat or fighting altogether.

What he did talk about was 12 Promises that a true practitioner of Brazilian Jiu Jitsu should make to his/her own self. Grand Master

Gracie believed – *and taught his students to believe* – that BJJ is a way of life in which fighting techniques are only part of the greater whole.

The central idea is for a person to be the best, most balanced, and most positive version of themself that it is possible to be. Here are Grand Master Gracie's "*12 Commandments of Brazilian Jiu Jitsu*" –

Promise yourself...

1. To be so secure that nothing can disturb your peace of mind.

2. To speak to all of happiness, health and prosperity.

3. To let your friends know that you value them.

4. To look at the bright side and turn your optimism into your reality.

5. To think only the best, work only for the best, and expect only the best.

6. To be as fair and as enthusiastic about the success of others as you are of your own.

7. To forget about past mistakes, and focus your energy on the achievements of the future.

8. To always make those around you happy, and smile when someone is talking to you.

9. To spend most of your time on self-improvement, and no time criticizing others.

10 .To be too complete to feel anxious, too noble to be angry, too happy to feel frustrated, and too strong to be fearful.

11. To have a good opinion of yourself, and proclaim it to the world. Not with loud words, but with good works.

12. To strongly believe that the world is on your side, as long as you stay loyal to your best self.

There's so much talk about "ground-fighting". What if I want to defend myself without getting on the ground?

If you are ever involved in a real-life fight, the odds are extremely high that at some point, one or both of you are going to be on the ground – just ask any law enforcement officer. Because Brazilian Jiu Jitsu is designed to help you prevail in the event of a real, violent confrontation, being proficient in ground-fighting techniques could mean the difference in winning or losing.

Also, remember – if your opponent has any sort of advantage – a weapon, size, greater strength – those advantages are usually negated when you're both on the ground. In fact, *on the ground*, your Brazilian Jiu Jitsu training and skill will give you a decided advantage over your attacker.

What should I look for in a good Brazilian Jiu Jitsu gym?

When you decide to begin training in Brazilian Jiu Jitsu, there are a multitude of factors that go into deciding on which school to attend. If you are new to the world of martial arts training, then it can be confusing to know exactly how to make the right choice.

When comparing different BJJ academies, there are several questions that you should be asking to determine if a particular school is right for you and if their approach is compatible with your goals.

- Can you set your own goals? In other words, are there different training paths for individuals who want to take up BJJ for fitness vs self-defense vs advancement to professional competition? Or do they have a "one-size-fits-all" approach?

- What are the qualifications are the instructors? There are three ways that BJJ instructors can earn the necessary certification –

  ➢ The Gracie Academy – Both Basic Certification and Advanced Instructor Training Is available. To even be certified as just a Level I Instructor, an applicant has to pass the blue belt test with a score of 90 or above, and *then* take an online course, and *then* an in-person training session at the company's headquarters in California.

  ➢ International Brazilian Jiu Jitsu Black Belt Instructors – Certified black belts are all automatically granted authorization to teach below their own level. For example, a black belt can only be given by someone who has earned the rank of second-degree black belt.

  In areas where there are not enough black belts to serve as instructors, brown or purple belts are allowed to serve in that capacity. Once again, they are still only allowed to teach below their own level.

  ➢ USA Jiu Jitsu Instructor Training Course – Held at various locations throughout the country, this three-day course grants participants a certificate and an instructor's stripe. They are allowed to teach students below their own rank.

  Remember, a certificate or a belt alone is not proof that a particular instructor is a *good* instructor. The best way to determine that is to sit in on classes and see how the instructor interacts with the students and how they respond to the teaching.

- **Is there a written curriculum and instruction?** Far too many so-called BJJ schools do not have an official "program" in place, and have virtually no established and trackable system to show how the students are progressing from one level to the next.

  A good Brazilian Jiu Jitsu school will have plans and goals in place to help you monitor your progress. There should be a step-by-step guide to show you what to expect, as well as to show what will be expected of you.

- **Is the facility clean, sanitary, and in good repair?** You might think that this is an obvious question, but the reality is that far too many facilities are cleaned infrequently or improperly. This means that you could run the risk of a serious infection from even a minor cut or abrasion.

  For that matter, ask about the school's protocol when there is an injury to a student and what the status of their liability insurance is. It is a simple fact of martial arts and sometimes injuries are going to happen, and you want to know that there is a plan in place to ensure that you are taking care.

- **Is there an introductory or "audit" period?** This is perhaps the very best way to determine if a particular Brazilian Jiu Jitsu school is right for you. The availability of this option is of real value to you, because the last thing you want to do is be locked in to an ironclad contract with a gym where you are uncomfortable.

What happens in a typical Brazilian Jiu Jitsu class?

Although each individual instructor will have his own specific way of instruction, the vast majority of Brazilian Jiu Jitsu classes will pretty much fall in line with a five-step in-class process.

- Warm-up – This will be a series of exercises designed to loosen/limber up the students. Calisthenics, stretches, two-person exercises, etc. may all be directed by the instructor or, more often, by a higher-level student. The warm-up helps prevent unnecessary injuries.

- Technique Instruction – This part of the class will be directed by the certified instructor. Usually only a few individual techniques are taught in a given class, typically, no more than two or three.

  The reason for this is twofold – first, if too many techniques are taught in one class, it may be difficult for some of the students to retain the information. Second, the students must be able to practice the technique over and over again to gain proficiency.

  Usually, the instructor will demonstrate the technique first, and then have the students drill the technique repeatedly. The instructor will watch each student and evaluate their execution of the technique.

Because it is a Brazilian Jiu Jitsu class, there will almost always be the teaching of some sort of take down or groundwork technique.

- <u>Position-Specific Sparring</u> – During this portion of class, students will begin a sparring session from a specific position, such as Closed Guard, Back-Mounted, etc. Since many of the taught techniques are designed to give the combatants into specific positions, this specific sparring will further teach the students actions to take and techniques to use once a favorable position has been achieved.

- <u>Free Sparring</u> – In longer advanced classes, students will face off against each other. For many, this is the most enjoyable part of the class, when they get to apply the skills and techniques they are learning.

- <u>The Warm-Down</u> – Similar to what was done beginning of class, the warm-down allows the students to stretch out any soreness and reduce the chance of any injury.

The Different Guards of Brazilian Jiu-Jitsu

The guard is a grappling position on the ground in which one combatant has their back to the ground while attempting to control the other combatant using their legs. In grappling combat martial arts, the guard is considered an advantageous position, because the bottom combatant can attack with various joint locks and chokeholds, while the combatant on top's priority is to transition into a more dominant position, known as passing the guard.

In MMA (Mixed Martial Arts) competition or hand-to-hand combat in general, it is possible to effectively strike from the top in the guard, even though the bottom combatant exerts some control. There are various types of guard, with their own advantages and disadvantages.

The guard is a key part of Brazilian Jiu-Jitsu (BJJ) where it can be used as an offensive position. It is also used, but not formally named, in judo though it is sometimes referred to as "do-osae" in Japanese, meaning "trunk hold". It is called the "front body scissor" in catch wrestling.

Pulling Guard

Pulling guard is so common place in Brazilian Jiu Jitsu that you see it in almost every competition video known to man. I have seen with the high level grapplers like Rousimar Palhares all the way down to children in their first ever competition.

However, I have seen it time-and-time again where someone pulls guard and just doesn't know what to do from there. Willingly pulling guard means that you have to be aggressive enough to work from this position, and not just sit there like a fish out of water.

When you should pull guard:

- Your opponent is a high level wrestler, or a Judo black belt.
- Your opponent is much bigger than you.

- You are injured and cannot fight on your feet.
- Strategy: your guard is much better than your top game.

Closed Guard

The closed guard is sometimes referred to as the full guard. The closed guard is the typical guard position. The legs are hooked behind the back of the opponent, preventing them from standing up or moving away. The opponent needs to open the legs up to be able to improve positioning. The bottom combatant might transition between the open and closed guard, as the open guard allows for better movement, but also there's an increased risk of the opponent passing the guard.

Open Guard

The open guard is typically used to perform various joint locks and chokeholds. The legs can be used to move the opponent, and to create leverage. The legs open allows the opponent to stand up or try to pass the guard, so this position is often used temporarily to set up sweeps or other techniques. Open guard is also a general term that encompasses a large number of guard positions where the legs are used to push, wrap or hook the opponent without locking the ankles together around them.

Butterfly Guard

The butterfly guard or hooks guard, in Portuguese: guarda de gancho(s) or guarda borboleta, is one of the oldest and most traditional forms of guard playing in jiu jitsu and is often labelled as a classic guard. The butterfly hooks are designed to jeopardize the base of the fighter with the top position (this being defined by the hind end off the ground and in most cases head above that of the guard player) using the bottom player's feet as hooks against the inside of the guard passer's legs.

The Butterfly Guard allows you to quickly attack your opponent with sweeps and transitions. The Butterfly Guard will also allow you to defeat a much larger and stronger opponent.

We will look at how to maintain the Butterfly Guard and how to attack from this unique position. In some BJJ circles, the Butterfly Guard is sometimes called Seated Guard because you are sitting up right as you try to launch your attacks.

Many people attempt to be offensive with their Butterfly Guard once they are on their backs. This is a very dangerous mistake. Unless you quickly transition to Half Guard or X Guard, you will probably get your Guard passed quickly.

It is much easier for your training partner to pass your Butterfly Guard once your shoulder blades are down on the mat. Remember, the Butterfly Guard is only offensive if you are sitting up. With the shoulder blades off the ground and sitting up like you are sitting at the beach.

It is extremely difficult to initiate a Sweep or a Submission from the Butterfly Guard once your shoulder blades are down on the mat. Often, when BJJ practitioners play the Butterfly Guard, they'll keep their feet on the mat and think that their knees and shins will keep them safe from the Guard Pass.

This is foolhardy and most people will find themselves in bottom cross side very quickly. The correct way to use your feet is to have them glued to your training partner's legs. At least one foot is touching your training partner's legs at all times. This does take awareness, sensitivity and practice, but it will make your Butterfly Guard much more difficult to pass.

From the Butterfly Guard, the most immediate attack from this position is to sweep your opponent. When attempting a Butterfly Guard Sweep, many people will keep both feet glued to the inside of their training partner's legs. Although this is a good tactic initially, one foot needs to be placed on the mat to help apply leverage for the sweep as the other foot lifts your training partner up for the sweep.

The foot that is placed on the mat has to be in a very specific spot: just outside of your training partner's knee. The moment you go for the sweep, if you have both your feet in between your training partner's legs, you need to bring your right foot underneath your left knee so that it will rest against the outside of your training partner's right knee.

Many people see the Butterfly Guard Sweep as a sweep done with one leg. They'll keep one leg on the mat while the other leg elevates their opponent; but, if their opponent has good balance and tries to defend the sweep, then the sweep is quickly nullified.

What you need to do is think of the Butterfly Guard Sweep as a 2 legged sweep – one leg elevates your training partner and the second leg drives aggressively into the mat. Doing the sweep this way is far more effective.

X-Guard

The x-guard is an open guard where one of the combatants is standing up and the other is on their back. The bottom combatant uses the legs to entangle one of the opponent's legs, which creates opportunities for powerful sweeps. The x-guard is often used in combination with butterfly and half guard. In a grappling match, this is an advantageous position for the bottom combatant, but in general hand-to-hand combat, the top combatant can attack with stomps or soccer kicks. Likewise, skilled use of the x-guard can prevent the opponent from attempting a kick, or throw them off balance should they raise a leg. The x-guard was popularised by Marcelo Garcia.

Spider Guard

The spider guard comprises a number of positions, all of which involve controlling the opponent's arms while using the soles of the feet to control the opponent at the biceps, hips, thighs, or a combination of them. It is most effective when the sleeves of the opponent can be grabbed, for instance if the opponent is wearing a gi. The spider guard can be used for sweeps and to set-up joint locks or chokeholds.

De la Riva Guard

The De la Riva guard (also called the De la Riva hook and Jello guard) is an open guard that was popularized in Brazilian Jiu-Jitsu by black belt Ricardo de la Riva Goded, who was successful with it in competition. In it, one of the legs is wrapped behind the opponent's leg from the outside, the ankle held with one hand,

and the other hand grips one of their sleeves. The De la Riva guard offers many sweeps, transitions and submissions, and is often used in combination with the spider guard.

Rubber Guard

The rubber guard is a grappling position of unknown origin that was first seen being put to use in competitions by Nino Schembri in the late 1990s, later being also picked up by Eddie Bravo in the early 2000s, who developed a training method heavily based on this particular situation. The rubber guard is a variation of the open guard where the guard player will grab his own shin with the opposite arm (example: right arm grabbing left shin) over his opponent's back, the grip should be performed with the palm of the hand facing upwards and the forearm should be in contact with the collarbone. These details will help the guard player keep his opponent's posture down, avoiding this way for the guard passer to pose an offence.

In MMA, and despite the position's main aim of helping Jiu Jitsu succeed in this environment, it seems to have fallen into a limbo. As the UFC evolved to shorter rounds with a scoring system that benefits striking, takedowns and top control on the ground, the rubber guard's efficiency in the sport was compromised, as it too often relies on time to work the top fighter into a submission.

50/50 Guard (Fifty – Fifty Guard)

The 50-50 (Fifty-fifty) guard is a position popularized by Roberto "Gordo" Correa and extensively used by the Mendes Brothers,

Rafael and Guilherme Mendes, Bruno Frazzato, Ryan Hall and Ramon Lemos from the Atos Jiu-Jitsu Team. In other grappling systems such as catch wrestling and Russian Sambo, it is a form of the "outside leg triangle" type of leg control. In this position, the fighter on the bottom crosses a triangle on the opponent's leg, which allows for the leg to be dominated while leaving the arms free to work on sweeps and submissions. This position has been heavily criticized for use in competitions with restricted use of leglocks due to the potential of stalling a match when the fighter on top cannot pass the guard and the fighter on the bottom cannot successfully perform a sweep.

I'm out of shape... I'm overweight... I'm older... Do I need to get "fit" before beginning Brazilian Jiu Jitsu?

As with any sport or exercise program, you should consult with your personal physician before beginning BJJ. If your doctor says that you're healthy enough to start, then by all means – START!

Beginner classes are a fantastic way to get back into shape. An experienced BJJ instructor will understand that many novice students aren't in the "best of shape", and even those students who think they are pretty fit probably aren't as ready as they think they are for the demands of Brazilian Jiu Jitsu.

Because of that, beginners are taught not only the basics of self-defense, but they will also get instruction in endurance, muscle-strengthening, flexibility, and cardio. Don't worry, if you're not in shape when you begin, you will definitely get there!

As for your age, don't let that discourage you either. There are numerous examples of well-known personalities within BJJ circles who didn't begin training until they were in their 60s... 70s... even their 80s!

The bottom-line is this – you are never too young, too old, too weak, or to overweight to start training in Brazilian Jiu Jitsu.

As a beginner, how often should I train?

How often a beginner should train can be answered a couple different ways. Obviously, how often you can train depends upon logistics – *your fitness level* (how much you can handle), *money* (how much you can afford), and *time* (your other commitments).

Let's make a couple of assumptions. Let's assume that your school is open every day of the week, let's assume that your fitness level is sufficient to allow you to attend that often, and let's finally assume that you can afford that many lessons.

We need to make those assumptions because if your school is only offers classes two days a week, if you have some health or fitness issue that limit you, or if attending extra classes just isn't in your budget, then your decision is already made for you.

That's okay – you do what you can, and bit by bit, you will improve.

No, let's answer this question by addressing the issue of time. Specifically, let's answer the question two ways –

What do you do if your time is limited (work, school, family obligations)?

And, what do you do if you have all the time you need to train – how much is enough?

If your time is limited, where you can only take one or two classes a week, that isn't ideal, but it is what you have to work with.

If you don't have a lot of time, then make up for it with effort and attention. Take lots of notes and refer to them on your off-training days. Pay extra attention and concentrate when you're instructor is demonstrating a technique. Most importantly, ask questions!

If you have all the time you need, then between two and four classes a week is probably your target frequency, as long as you can be consistent. You don't want to over-train to the point where you either get burned out or injured, especially here at the beginning when you aren't used to this level of physical exertion.

And here's the bottom-line when it comes to attendance – quality is infinitely preferable to quantity. If you can only come once a week, be the best student at that particular class.

Is Brazilian Jiu Jitsu right for women?

Because BJJ teaches fighting techniques designed to neutralize any advantages in reach, size, or power that an attacker might have, it is an especially useful for martial arts discipline for women. Many women report that when the benefits of their training helps them realize that they are no longer vulnerable because of their smaller stature, they are able to go about their lives with much more confidence and self-assurance.

Comparatively speaking, there are currently far fewer women engaged in Brazilian Jiu Jitsu training when there are men. Realistically, this means that it is far more likely that when a woman spars during training, she will have to pair off against a man.

However, for practical purposes, this is a good thing, because it gets them into the habit of using BBJ techniques against a larger opponent. If she is ever faced with a real-life situation, she will already have you experience and the muscle-memory that will aid her self-defense.

A Quick Guide to Rolling (Sparring)

As stated earlier, a large part of your Brazilian Jiu Jitsu training will be dedicated to sparring, or as it is called within the sport, rolling.

For the sake of safety and education, let's go over a few of the most basic rules governing rolling, as well as some of the more common allowable/illegal techniques.

When sparring in class, it is not customary to go all-out with 100% effort. The reason behind this is that the goal is the proper execution of the technique, rather than defeating your sparring opponent. Since you're there to learn, the idea is that if you are not going 100%, you can concentrate on performing maneuver correctly.

Usually, a lessened effort of approximately 50% to 75% is allowable.

Along those same lines, rolling in class is not a competition. In other words, do not actually "battle" your opponent, attempting to win at all costs. Again, learning the technique is the goal, so expect the flow of your instruction to go back and forth. If during a particular exercise you are submitted, do not become overly frustrated, because it is all part of the training.

One of the first and most important skills you need to learn when you begin rolling is about how to both tap out and how to respond to a tap. Because this is a simple movement that will protect both you and your opponent from serious injury, it is of paramount importance that you are always aware of when it is time for you to tap, and when it is time for you to tap out yourself.

Here are a couple of ironclad, mandatory rules about tapping.

- ALWAYS tap with your free hand, and ALWAYS tap with enough force that your opponent will feel it.
- ALWAYS tap your opponent's body, never the mat, because your opponent may neither hear nor notice it, resulting in a serious injury to you.
- If your hands are trapped, tap your legs on the mat, hard.
- When you are tapping, call out loudly and clearly, "TAP!"
- ALWAYS tap out as soon as you begin to feel the submission technique's affect. DO NOT wait until the last second.
- Make an effort never to cry out in pain unless you are intending to tap.
- Protect your opponent, as your opponent will protect you – pay attention and immediately stop if they tap.

For safety's sake, various moves/techniques fall into different categories and must be used accordingly – Legal, Illegal, and Legal for Higher Belts.

Legal Moves – These moves are always allowed during rolling, and require no permission.

- Blood chokes – putting pressure on the *sides* of your opponent's neck
- Elbow locks – this includes all armbars
- Shoulder locks
- Crossfacing – directly pushing your opponent's face

Legal, but Frowned upon – These moves are technically legal, but discouraged, because there are better ways to accomplish the same goal. They are considered to be in poor taste – the moves of a beginner.

- Combination chokes/neck cranks
- Hard crossfacing
- Choking the face/jaw
- Smothering
- Use of pressure points

Illegal Moves – These moves are not allowed in any level of Brazilian Jiu Jitsu competition. NEVER use these techniques, even if they are used against you in competition.

- Neck cranks – bending the neck to put pressure on the spine
- Twisting leg locks/heel hooks – twisting your opponent's foot
- Body-slamming – picking your opponent up and throwing them back down
- Manipulation of small joints – putting pressure on your opponent's toes or fingers
- Reaping of the knee – holding your opponent's leg stationary and bending the knee inward
- Attacking the windpipe

Legal for Higher Belts – These moves are legal for higher belts in Brazilian Jiu Jitsu competitions, and allowable with permission in some schools.

- Kneebars – bending the knee straight back

- <u>Straight ankle locks</u> – bending the ankle straight back
- <u>Wrist locks</u> – twisting or straight attacks on your opponent's wrist
- <u>Slicers</u> – putting pressure on your opponent's elbow or knee around another limb
- <u>Toe holds</u> – bending the foot into a "figure-four" hold

What can I do if I get tired very quickly during sparring?

It is very common for beginners at Brazilian Jiu Jitsu to become fatigued quickly during sparring, even if they are in excellent shape. This is due to a couple of reasons.

The first reason is simple anxiety. When a new practitioner is just starting out, it's very easy to become overly-excited And over-adrenalized. When this is the case, it's hard to stay relaxed and maintain a correct breathing pattern. And no breath equals no oxygen equals fatigue.

The second reason is inexperience. A new fighter will use more energy than a veteran and tried to use brute strength, rather than positioning, leverage, and technique. Trying to wrestle with your opponent can be exhausting.

When either of these happens to you, simply... relax.

That's it – relax, focus on your breathing, and conserve energy by fighting a technically-sound fight. Pick your moments, and choose the best time to apply your sparring, rather than extending it all at once.

Beyond that, the other obvious answer is to do extra work on your cardio and conditioning routine.

I'm scared of being injured during sparring. What should I do?

There is no way to sugar-coat this – injuries do happen in Brazilian Jiu Jitsu. That is a reasonable expectation in a combat sport. However, there are some common-sense measures you can take to minimize your chances of being injured.

First, always train under the supervision of a qualified instructor. Always pay strict attention during training to all of your teacher's instructions, because it is their job and their professional obligation to keep you as safe as possible.

Another thing you can do to minimize the chance of injury is to leave your ego at the door when you're sparring with someone in your Brazilian Jiu Jitsu school. Remember, sparring is a time to learn, practice, and perfect the techniques and movements that you're being taught.

Sparring _is not_ a time to belittle or talk down to your opponent, nor is it a time to try to make up for past insults. This is not a real fight, it is a sparring session, and if both you and your opponent can just remember that simple fact, you are less likely to get injured.

Finally, remember that it is the obligation of both you and your sparring partner to protect each other. Since the purpose of a sparring match is to learn, there is no need to go all-out and attempting to win at any cost, including deliberately or negligently entering your opponent.

That courtesy extends in both directions.

I see that a lot of BJJ practitioners have "cauliflower ear", and that worries me. How can I avoid it?

First, it's important to understand exactly what "cauliflower ear" is, and how it is caused.

The condition is caused when a person's ear is struck a blow that rips the cartilage away from the perichondrium. The injury fills up with liquid, and if not drained, the liquid can eventually harden into a fibrous lump.

The injury can result from one heavy blow, a lesser number of solid blows, or the result of extended damage over time.

The absolute best way to protect against cauliflower ear is to wear protective equipment, such as ear guards. Unfortunately, in some competitions, protective equipment for the head is prohibited.

The important thing to remember if any injury along these lines occurs, seek medical attention as soon as possible. A doctor can drain the excess fluid so the damage can heal itself, provided it's gotten to soon enough. If you delay, the condition can become permanent.

I'm getting frustrated because I'm not progressing fast enough... How can I overcome my frustration?

The first thing you need to do is realize that the frustration you feel is extremely common among beginners.

When most beginners initially start training, their excitement and enthusiasm can barely be contained. Later, when they realize the physical commitment, they start having to experience what it's like to tap out on a daily basis, and worst of all, when they start comparing their progress to that of others, that enthusiasm can turn into bitterness and frustration.

Once again, the feeling is extremely common.

There are some mental shifts – changes in the way you might be looking at things – that have proven to be quite helpful.

First, stop comparing yourself to other people. Although Brazilian Jiu Jitsu is a combat sport and there are competitions that recognizes both winners and losers, the only real yardstick by which you should be measuring yourself is – yourself.

Many newcomers to Brazilian Jiu Jitsu try to judge their progress against their peers, invariably without having all of the information. You have no idea if the other person has more time to train, any previous experience, more natural athleticism, etc., so comparing yourself to others gives an incomplete picture of how you are doing.

Instead, compare your self today against the "you" of back when you started. If you have improved at all, then you are doing just fine.

Another simple technique to avoid frustration is to focus on the learning of new techniques, rather than simply wins and losses. Every time you master a new technique, you have just gained a personal victory, with no chance of defeat.

Some Basic Effective Techniques for BJJ

Have you ever wondered what the most popular and powerful BJJ techniques are? Here's our list of the top submissions taught in BJJ gyms all over the world.

WARNING: not all of these techniques are legal in competition, or allowed at all gyms. But it's still better to be familiar with these illegal techniques just in case someone tries to use them on you. And many of these illegal BJJ moves still have a ton of validity for MMA applications or self defense situations, so they are well worth learning!

1. Guillotine Choke

The gullotine choke is a major submission move that is regularly applied when you're standing or in the closed guard position. There are numerous variations of the Choke, including the Marcelotine, the Arm- in and the 10 Finger choke.

How to perform this move:

a) **Bend your opponent over.**

Snap their head down. The point is to get their head down to your chest.

b) **Wrap your arm around the neck.**

Their neck has to be set between your lower arm and bicep.

c) **Pull your opponent's neck down to your hip and arm.**

This will put a lot of weight on their neck.

d)   If your opponent tries to take you down to the ground, wrap your legs around their body as soon as you touch the ground.

e)   **Keep applying similar pressure as a sleeper hold.**

This will either incapacitate them or force a tap out.

Videos of the Gullotine Choke

Marcelotine: https://youtu.be/2ortF7sjrrc

Guillotine   from   Closed   Guard: https://youtu.be/DLrXGWLtOoU

Standing Guillotine: https://youtu.be/nCCVE3zQfqc

Arm-in Guillotine Choke: https://youtu.be/QQQpUM8Q20s

2.   Rear Naked Choke

The Rear Naked Choke is also called the sleeper hold, which is one of the most critical submissions in BJJ. This move is the most elegant approach to end a fight.

How to perform this move:

a)   **Get behind your opponent and drop them to the ground.**

The rear naked choke, as the name suggests, makes it necessary that you are behind your opponent. While the hold can also be performed from the standing position, it is recommended to drop your opponent to the ground for better control and a better chance of finishing the submission.

b) **Wrap your legs around them, so that your insteps are within their thighs or knees.**

At the same time, put one arm over their neck and towards the focal point of the chest, while placing your other arm under your opponent's. Fasten your hands together in a tight grasp over the chest in what is known as the seat belt.

c) **Release the seat belt and put one arm around your opponent's neck.**

This would probably be the upper arm of the seat belt position but it doesn't make any difference. Attempt to get your elbow against thier chin, so that the throat is on the inside of your elbow. The arm around the opponent's neck will consequently be referred to as your "main hand", while the free arm is dubbed as your "off hand".

d) **Use your main hand to grab the bicep of the off hand.**

The grasp is frequently called as the "figure four", because of the way your arms shape the number 4 when performing it. This can serve as a rule in case you are uncertain on how you ought to hold your opponent.

e) **Keep the figure-four hold in place.**

Place your off hand of the moment against the back of your opponent's neck, to the point where it's attached to the arm that is circled around the neck. For reasons that will be examined below, it is advisable that you make a fist, as it won't be grabbing anything for the rest of the hold.

f) **Squeeze.**

Gradually, flex the arm that is choking as much as you can, while pushing your off hand into your opponent's neck from behind. If the choke is executed properly, it will interrupt the blood stream to the brain, bringing about unconsciousness in just about 4 to 5 seconds.

Videos of the Rear Naked Choke

Basic RNC: https://youtu.be/176SLdBhj_A

RNC Trick: https://youtu.be/-ciTiubaFa8

RNC – The most common errors:
https://youtu.be/K5IVkWszO8U

Bas Rutten's RNC: https://youtu.be/LppnEfRoFIM

3. Triangle Choke

The Triangle Choke is a signature move in grappling and it has brought a lot of sparring sessions and matches to an end. The Triangle Choke can be a difficult submission move and it can take a while to master the finer points that make this choke so effective. Be that as it may, if you have long and flexible legs, then this may very well be your signature move.

How to perform this move:

a. **Begin by laying on your back with your legs separated.**

Your opponent's waist should be in the middle of your legs. This is called "open guard" as their movements are somewhat limited by your legs but not as much as they would be if your legs were wrapped around his middle or in the "closed guard" position.

b) At this time, as your opponent is caught inside your guard, they will be attempting to use their elbows while searching for a way to break your guard. To start setting up your triangle choke you need to get one of the arms as they are attempting to open your guard and divert it so it moves to the side of your head instead of hitting it. Once this is achieved you should make every effort to hold the now extended arm locked in this position.

c) **Pull yourself into position.**

When your opponent's attack has been diverted and their arm is locked it is time to position your own body. You do this by using your legs to push your body so that your opponent is far from your head. With some practice you ought to have the capacity to position your body at the same time as protecting yourself from any manoeuvring attempts or attacks from the remaining arm.

d) **Pivot your hips forward.**

This will force your opponent's body to slide further down yours.

e) You now need to figure out how to manoeuvre one of your legs over the arm of your opponent that was pushed down and far from you.

f) **Begin to raise your legs above and over your opponent's head.**

At this time you should be in a position where your opponent's head is between your hips. You should also still maintain a firm hold of their arm at the side of your head. It's time to begin raising your legs up and over your opponents head. You need to start wrapping one leg around your opponent's head and shoulders making constantly sure that their arm is still caught between their own neck and head. Bring your foot towards your other leg.

g) **Wrap your knee around the feet of your other leg securing your opponent's immobilization.**

Use your shin to position your leg over your opponent's back to facilitate the choke, but do not put pressure on your foot as this can cause you to break your shin or dislocate your ankle.

h) **Using your legs you need to apply as much pressure as you can to the neck and head of your opponent.**

You will notice that gradually your opponent's arm that is locked against the neck limits the airflow to the lungs of your opponent. You can use one of your hands to pull down on the head which will apply significantly more pressure which will bring faster tap for the choke.

i) Hold the choke until your opponent either taps out, the referee stops the battle, or your opponent is incapacitated.

Videos of Triangle Chokes

Basic Triangle Choke: https://youtu.be/IwN-E7LO3bM

5 Triangle Chokes you must know: https://youtu.be/FbXunEbkf8E

Triangle Choke Mount: https://youtu.be/gc5YRdv-wSw

The 4 most common errors: https://youtu.be/9yfi5N1O3dA

4. Kimura / Keylock

The Kimura is an effective arm lock that is performed against your opponent's arm at the level of their chest and in front, focusing on the shoulder and elbow joints.

How to perform this grip:

a)   Take your opponent in the closed guard position.

b)   To break their stance pull their body into yours with your legs as you use your hands to push their arms out to the side.

c)   Now grab their right wrist with your left hand, open your feet, and sit up toward that arm to secure it into the Kimura position (wrapping around your opponent's arm with your right arm and grabbing your own wrist).

d)   To complete the grip, lie back to the floor and move into your opponent while pushing their hips away. Put your right foot to their left side hip, through your left leg high above their upper back, and get the submission.

Videos of the Kimura

Traditional Kimura: https://youtu.be/HA-2NRuTLkw

Kimura from Guard: https://youtu.be/xqSdVL82QVk

Kimura from Side Control:
https://youtu.be/QT0TqceznpQ

Kimura - 3 Most Common Errors:
https://youtu.be/nJotiTewRbl

Standing Kimura: https://youtu.be/SnLuzJi23MA

Sakuraba style Kimuras: https://youtu.be/Ly11uw2l-80

5. Ude Garami (aka Americana / V Armlock)

This technique is one of the first ones you learn in most grappling arts. It is a twisting grip that most of the time focuses on the shoulder joint, resulting in a submission, a bone break, or a dislocation .

How to execute:

a) Put your opponent on his back. Hold your opponent's lower arm with both hands so his wrist is twisted upwards and facing outwards.

b) Position your legs so that your knees are twisted in such a way that your opponent's arm and elbow is positioned between your legs.

c) Kick both of your feet upwards while pulling on his arm to draw both bodies while keeping the arm positioned wrist up. The outcome should be to find your groin under or near your opponent's shoulder.

d) Wrap both legs over his chest (one on every side of the arm) while maintaining their elbow straight to force their wrist towards you.

e) Using your opponent's chest as support, pull their wrist towards your chest and apply upward pressure using your hips. It won't take long before the technique compels your opponent to tap out.

Videos of the Americana:

Americana: https://youtu.be/SlPrqwwiaOY

High Percentage Americana: https://youtu.be/VOiFJf8VrZI

Josh Barnett Americana: https://youtu.be/g1eSGYM0QbQ

Americana and Kimura: https://youtu.be/vjNXcnmZ7wg

6. Armbar

When you apply the Inverse Armbar you trap your opponent's wrist between your own head and shoulder and apply pressure onto his elbow using your arms. This submission is normally accompanied by a knee mount or a close guard position.

How to execute this move:

a) Get your opponent in a closed guard position.

b) Secure the right sleeve of your opponent with your left hand. Cross grab their right elbow with your right hand. As you grab the arm, lift your hips off the floor to apply more power into the arm pulling process.

c) Pull their arm over and secure their chest and legs. Meanwhile open both legs and through them upwards in a crossing manner.

d) Immediately close your legs and lock your opponent's shoulder up to keep them from getting away.

e) Squeeze both knees to one side and cross your opponent's face with their hand so that they become defensless.

f) Place your left leg over your opponent's face and pull your hips upwards while controlling the arm. The technique is complete and your opponent must submit.

Video of Armbar:

Ronda Rousey Armbar: https://youtu.be/3lXdVDJxDg4

10 ways to finish the Armbar: https://youtu.be/8wNQ5UGLQHk

Armbar from Mount: https://youtu.be/ECPcvbKt-lY

7. Omoplata

The omoplata comes from the Greek word «ωμοπλάτη» which means scapula. The technique can force your opponent to tap out, however depending on their response, you can either incapacitate and get the submission, or achieve a favorable position for other submission techniques (such as taking the back and getting a rear naked choke).

How to execute the technique:

a) Execute an 'armbar' technique against your opponent from the guard position.

b) If your opponent manages to get away from your arm grip, raise your hips and open your knees to keep them from getting away altogether. Use your right hand to add more pressure and twist your opponent's left arm to one side.

c) Bring your right hand to your opponent's belt and your left hand to their trousers. Lock your legs in a figure four position around your opponent's shoulder to get yourself into position.

d) To defend thesmelves, your opponent will probably turn into you by raising their head. Open your legs and keep your hips high to maintain your position.

e) Place your right foot onto your opponent's left hip and kick your left leg over the back of his neck while pulling his arm toward you.

f) To get the submission, close your legs in the triangle position, lift your hips and choke the head.

Video of Omoplatas:

Omoplata: https://youtu.be/LVy4tGv5Fk4

4 ways to Improve your omoplata:
https://youtu.be/5mwTslcGH1Y

8. Gogoplata

The Gogoplata is a variation of the Omoplata technique for flexible fighters. To apply it you weave the foot that traps your opponent's arm around their throat, then press the foot into the throat to complete the choke.

How to execute the technique:

a) Drop your opponent to the floor, and bring him in the guard position on top of your body.

b) Grab your opponent's hand or arm that is parallel to your right arm and pull it toward your left shoulder.

c) As you force the arm put your right leg under your jaw, so that your shin and lower leg is against your opponent's neck or throat.

d) Bring the opponent's arm that you grabbed in step 2 to the area of your abdomen and release it.

e) Place your left leg against your opponent's neck so that your legs form an "h".

f) Put your hands behind your opponent's head and draw it toward your legs.

Videos of the Gogoplata:

Regular Gogoplata: https://youtu.be/uTKDmjU88Jc

No-Gi Gogoplata: https://youtu.be/pFZxBSa1vLY

Gogplata from Mount: https://youtu.be/MnauxGlVm2g

9. Figure 4 Toehold

You may have seen your most favourite wrestling stars performing the figure four leg lock on TV, and now you have decided to attempt it yourself. This move can be an awesome approach in the battle with your opponent, yet it is important that it is executed correctly. Keep reading so that you may learn how to do so.

How to execute the technique:

a) First of all, make sure that your opponent is lying flat on the ground before you can begin executing the technique.

b) Grab his right leg and put your left leg over it, so that you are facing away from your opponent.

c) Then grab their left leg and bend the other one until their right foot rests on their left leg over the knee. Face to one side of your opponent. At this point your opponent's legs should be forming a kind of a "P", or a "4" shape with your right leg forming the tail of it.

d) Hold that position and fall back. You'll need to twist a bit in the right, so that you can lay on your back. Make sure that you are at the opposite side of your opponent and not facing him.

e) To complete the technique, take your left leg and place it over your opponent's foot.

f) If is possible to modify the technique and execute it in reverse. The difference in this variation is that you need to make your opponent lay on their back and place their left leg underneath your thigh.

g) Then push their right leg up hard until their left foot comes beneath their thigh. Keep pushing forward but not too hard.

Videos of the toehold:

Toehold: https://youtu.be/o8jrAKnGqnw

Basic Toehold: https://youtu.be/1lYsi1Y-rGY

Toehold Variation: https://youtu.be/mFno2NYeaJl

Toehold to tap Larger Opponents: https://youtu.be/hLef63326MA

Not all of the above techniques are legitimate for execution in a competition. However, they are permitted and taught in all gyms. Legitimacy aside, you should be familiar with these illegal texhniques should the case be that someone tries to use them on you.

Another reason to learn the aforementioned techniques is that they are still valid as far as self defense is concerned and for various MMA applications. Just make sure they are properly and well executed.

Competing in your first BJJ tournament

First you need to ask your instructor if you are ready to compete. Some schools encourage competition for students with as little as one month of experience. Others would prefer if their students trained for several months and exhibited a level of skill where the coaches are comfortable with letting them compete. It is important to consult with your coaches since they will be an integral part of helping you prepare for the tournament and since you will be representing your gym and instructor in the competition.

Find out the Brazilian Jiu-Jitsu tournament schedule for the area where you live. Once your coaches give the green light for competing, the next step is finding out which tournaments are coming up and which ones would be the right fit for you to make your debut. There are the organized tournaments run by organizations such as NAGA, IBJJF, NABJJF, and Five Grappling to name a few. These tournament entry fees usually cost between $50 and $100 (£30 and £70) to enter a tournament. There are also smaller local and in-house tournaments run at local high schools and martial arts schools that costs between $10 and $50 (£5 and £30) to enter and could offer both single and double elimination formats so you can get more experience at these events. Also, check with your coaches to see if they are aware of any upcoming tournaments that might be a good fit for you.

Make sure you have enough time to prepare

Give yourself 6 to 8 weeks to prepare for the tournament. If you are going to compete in your first tournament, giving yourself the proper amount of time to prepare so you can perform to the best of your ability will be extremely important. Of course, you can sign up for a tournament at the last minute. But if you want to reach your full potential, giving yourself adequate time to prepare will be very important.

Getting registered

Most tournaments offer online registration. When you register, you will need to enter your contact information, BJJ gym name, and, division/weight class. Ask your coaches what you should enter as your gym name since some schools might enter tournaments under their affiliation name rather than their gym name.

Choosing the right weight class

Choosing a weight class is another area where you should consult with your coaches. You first need to find out whether the weigh-ins are right before your match, the day before, or morning of your tournament and whether you weigh-in with or without your gi on, which can add as much as 4 to 6 pounds to your weight. Also, if you are just 3 to 5 pounds above your weight class, you will need to consult with your coaches to decide whether you should cut down to the next weight class. With an increased training schedule and proper diet, dropping the extra weight might not be too difficult. But this will depend on your body type.

Pick a realistic and comfortable weight class to achieve to help reduce any stress during your training and to make sure your body is fully energized throughout your training camp.

Most tournaments offer different age divisions for adults divisions. The most popular and biggest division is the adult division for competitors between 18 and 30 years in age. You can be a 40 year old and still compete in the adult division if you are looking for a challenge. For competitors above 30 years of age, there are various 'masters' divisions broken into 5 year age blocks such as 31 to 35, 36 to 40, etc. If you are 37 years old, and have no one in your weight class, then you can drop down to the 31 to 35 Masters division or the adult division.

Always read the rules

Also, when you register, read over the rules, scoring system, and find the tournament's competitor 'check date.' The 'check date' is usually 5 to 7 days before the tournament where competitors are able to email the tournament promoters to change weight classes and divisions. You may want to consider changing weight classes and divisions if you are not sure you would make weight for the weight class you initially signed up for and if there isn't anybody else signed up for your weight class/division. For some smaller tournaments, the promoters might also choose to combine weight classes and divisions if there aren't enough competitors registered (this happens more than you might think).

Ask questions

Speak to your coaches about your training schedule. Your coaches and your training partners will be your best friends during your training camp leading up to your first tournament. Talk to the coaches about your training schedule and whether you need to increase the amount of time you spend on the mat each week or start attending competition team classes (if your gym has those classes). If you are going to reach out to your coaches and teammates to help you prepare for a tournament, you should follow their advice and speak with them if you have any reservations or if you can't follow through on the training schedule laid out for you.

Diet to Cut Weight

In order for you to reach your potential and perform at your best, make sure you are eating a healthy diet and getting 7 to 8 hours of sleep each night. While there are many different diet plans out there such as the Ketagenic Diet, Dolce Diet or Paleo Diet for Athletes, the basic principles of any a healthy diet plan would be to cut out processed foods, focus on whole foods, reduce or eliminate gluten and processed sugars in the diet, and consume healthy fats and proteins.

Game Planning

It is important to go into your tournament with a basic game plan that you have drilled and practiced in rolling and sparring during your training camp leading up to your first tournament. The game plan should be very basic and account for an escape from bad positions and 1 to 2 moves from each position. For instance, have a takedown and a guard pull from the standing position, have an escape if you are mounted, have 2 escapes from bottom side control, and 2 guard passes from closed and open guard. When you are developing a game plan, you also need to take into account that you could be competing in up to 3 to 5 matches on the day.

The game plan should also factor in energy expenditure for multiple matches. If you have a very fast paced style, ask yourself if you can sustain that style over multiple matches. Again, you should consult with your coaches on your game plan and decide which moves should be included in your game plan. Once you start developing the game plan, drill the moves during open mats and use those moves during your rolls. Also, visualize your perfect match each day where all of the moves in your game plan mentally flow together.

Your training partners are your best friends when it comes to competition

In addition to your coaches, your training partners will be a big part of your preparation. Finding training partners in your weight class that can help you with drilling, rolling, and practicing your game plan will be very important for you success. Be proactive and ask specific training partners if they can attend specific open mats and training sessions to help you prepare. If you are a heavyweight and the only other teammates that show up for an open mat or training session are all a 150 lbs, it might not be as productive as if you had other heavyweights to work with on that day.

Keep checking your weight

Monitor your weight and how you feel. Constantly check your weight by weighing yourself every morning right after you wake up and use the bathroom. This will help give you an idea of whether you are on track for making weight. It is important to have an accurate scale. Buying a higher end, durable digital scale for $40 can remove many potential headaches.

Listen to your body

With the increase in mat time and proper nutrition, your body is basically a living chemistry experiment. Monitor how you are feeling. Make notes each day on your workouts, diet, and whether you feel fresh or tired and sluggish. You want to prevent overtraining and burn out. If your resting pulse rate increases or if you are feeling sore and inflamed, you might be overtraining. If this is the case, consult with your coaches to see if you can cut back on the amount and intensity of your training while still preparing for the tournament. There is no shame in scaling back your training in order to aid in recovery and prevent overtraining.

Visualization

Take time out during each day and think about your game plan and visualize your perfect match from start to finish in your head. Think with intent on what your set ups will be, how you will execute your moves, how you will transition from position to position to submission. Also, visualize yourself being mounted or having your back taken and walk yourself through the steps of how you will escape. This is a 5 to 10 minute exercise each day that can be done in silence, in the shower, during your drive to work or whenever works for you.

The week of the tournament

You have made it through 5 to 7 weeks of training and preparation for your tournament. Now you only have 5 to 7 days before the big game. Here are some key points to consider in the days leading up to the tournament.

How is your weight?

Are you on weight or over weight for your weight division? If it is 1 to 3 pounds, be honest and ask yourself if you can drop the weight without much strain to your body. If not, just go up a weight class for this tournament. You do not need the mental and physical stress of making weight during the week of your first tournament (regardless of what coaches and training partners say). If you do choose to go up a weight class, you will have the freedom to consume more calories from healthy, whole foods which will aid in your preparation and recovery leading up to the big day.

The check day

This is the date we previously talked about where you can change your weight division. Many tournaments will list the competitors and allow you to view how many people are in your division. The amount of people in your division might persuade you to move up a weight class or down to an age division with more competitors.

Check the schedule

Find out the schedule/bracket. The brackets and schedule will usually be released 1 to 3 days prior to the tournament. This will let you know when you are scheduled to compete and how many people will be in your bracket.

Let everyone know when you are competing

Let your coaches know when you are competing and find out which coach will be there to corner you. Also, let your teammates, friends, and family know what time you will be competing. Text or email them the time and venue address and let them know you might not be able to respond to text messages on the day of the tournament since you will be prepping and warming up. Having people in your corner is a great source of positive energy and will provide an extra boost for you on your big day. It can make a big difference.

Plan the day out

Layout your whole day based on when you will be competing including when you will be arriving at the venue, your warm up routine, what time you wake up, test weigh-ins, scenarios based on whether you are on or over weight, what you will eat, when you will eat. Also pack your gym bag the night before as it will be one less thing to worry about.

Get there early

If you are competing in the morning at 9 or 10 AM, get to the venue by 6:30 AM. For some tournaments, the competitor check in line could take as long as 1 hour to get through. Getting to the venue early and to the front of the line will help remove any distractions and headaches. The morning of the tournament is valuable time to rest, get focused, and warm up. Waiting in a long line to check-in will take a mental and physical toll on the body since you are feeling stressed and anxious on time and you are standing up while waiting in line for up to an hour.

Weight and diet

Depending on where your weight stands, you may need to closely monitor your caloric intake. It is important to keep eating and drinking in the days leading up to the tournament even if you are above your weight class's limit. Just watch your portion sizes, cut out salt and the carbohydrates from starches. Also, do not introduce anything new into your diet that hasn't been in your diet during your training camp. Eating something foreign like curry or fried chicken could upset your stomach and weaken your body. Work with your coaches and have a plan at least 2 weeks out on how to maintain and manage your weight during the week leading up to the tournament.

Taper down your training

5 to 7 days before your tournament everything will likely already be done. All of the game plan implementation should be squared away. Your cardio should be ready for the big day. Now it is time

to cut back on your workouts and let your body recover so that it will be as close as possible to 100% on the day of the tournament. At this point, there should not be any more hard workouts. Workouts should be light and focused on drilling and flowing through your game plan. You can train every day or every other day, but the workouts should be light and focused on technique in order to recover and avoid any risks of injuries. This is another area where you should consult with your coaches on how to taper down properly.

The day of the tournament

The big day is here. All of the hard work, training, and sacrifice have gotten you to this point. Here are a few things to remember for the big day.

Weigh yourself

Weigh yourself right when you wake up. Weigh yourself in or out of your gi based on the tournament weigh-in rules and eat and drink an amount of food and liquid that will keep you on weight and energized. Weigh yourself again each time after you eat and drink just so you know where you stand.

Know where the venue is

Know the address of your venue, where the parking is located, and where you can potentially warm up. Many venues have very cramped warm up areas with limited space. If there is a soccer field or track close to the venue, you can warm up there by running laps, stretching, and doing calisthenics without the noise and having potential opponents stare at you. Looking up the venue on Google Maps on your phone can give you an idea of potential outdoor warm up areas you can use.

Pack an extra Gi just in case

Before you compete, check with your coaches to make sure the gis are approved for competition and all of the patches are sewed on in legal areas of the gi. Part of the weigh-in process is the gi check and they will make sure that the gi is the correct material, length on the arms and legs, and patches are only in the allowed areas of the gi. Packing an extra gi will also save you in case your gi top or pants rip during your matches.

Bring food and water

Bring plenty of water. Your matches will drain you and if you have multiple matches, you want to make sure you have enough water in your gym bag to avoid dehydration and cramping during your matches. Also, pack light snacks to eat before your matches if you are on weight. Raisins, fresh fruit, nuts, and tracker bars are healthy options that won't upset the stomach and provide sustaining energy for your matches.

Bring ID

You will need to have your ID card to check in to the tournament, when you weigh-in, and for the scorekeeper's table next to your mat. So keep it handy and accessible in your bag or have it on a lanyard. Just don't forget it at home.

Bring music that will help to get you in the zone

An iPod can be a life saver on your competition day. Having music can help get you in the right mood, help you warm up, and channel out all of the noise in the bullpen when you are waiting to compete. Create a play list of songs that get you pumped up and ready for battle.

Pack a sweat shirt and pants

A hoodie sweat shirt and dri-fit gear will come in handy if you need to cut some weight and during your warm up. Warming up initially in a sweat suit instead of a gi will prevent your gi from getting weighed down by sweat especially if you have to weigh-in in the gi. Once you are warmed up, change into your gi for the weigh-ins.

Arrive early

Arriving early will help alleviate any stress from potential traffic jams and long check-in lines, and allow you to get acclimated to the venue. Some competitors like to arrive as a team and watch other competitors compete before their own matches. Others, who are close to weight, prefer to rest at home and arrive just in time for their own matches. It comes down to your own team's policies and your preferences that day.

Weigh-in again

Right when you arrive at the venue, weigh-in to see where you stand. If you are on or underweight, rest and relax. If you are slightly overweight, you will need to go for a short run or skip with a jump rope to get your weight down.

Have a warm up planned out

Know your body and what type of warm up routine works best for you. Talk to your coach about how and when you should warm up for a tournament. This is highly overlooked, especially at the white-belt level. You want to make sure you are sweating and past your first wind by the time you step on the mat for your first match.

Have someone film you

Make sure you have a friend and family member available to record your matches. Also give them clear directions on how to operate your camera or phone just to avoid getting your matches recorded in portrait format, when you wanted them recorded in landscape or not recorded at all.

Be respectful

When you are on deck at your mat, do not enter the mat until the referee signals for you to step on the mat. Bow towards the referee before stepping on the mat. Shake the referee's hand as well as your opponent's hand. Before the match starts, bow towards your opponent and you can extend your hand to slap hands and fist bump. During the match, do not speak to your opponent or the referee. This can result in a penalty or a disqualification. Once the match is over, bow and shake hands with your opponent and the referee again and bow towards the mat before stepping off of it.

Your opponent's grips will feel strong

Competing in a tournament and rolling in class are two completely different animals. The adrenaline and excitement from both you and your opponent will be very apparent when you grip fight. Your opponent's grips will feel like the grips of a giant silverback gorilla. Stay calm and remember what you trained in practice and what you must do. Remember your techniques and have fun out there.

Make sure you go to the podium

Some tournaments have a match to determine the third place finishers. Others award two third place medals. If you do lose in the semi-finals, stick around until the end and go to the podium to receive your medal. It is very disrespectful to the other competitors who made the podium to no show the medal ceremony at the podium. Go to the podium for the picture and congratulate your fellow competitors for a job well done.

Learning is the most important thing

There is no losing in martial arts, only winning and learning. If the day didn't go your way, it doesn't matter. Review your matches, take notes and share what you did well and what you found difficult with your coach. Learn from the mistakes you made in your preparation and your matches and work to refine them. Use the experience to grow and get better, regardless of the outcome.

If the day did not go your way, do not get discouraged. Just go back to the mats next week and continue training and having fun. That is the most important thing.

Coming Back from an Injury

There are two certainties in BJJ. Eventually you will become addicted to it. At some point you will experience some type of injury. I wish the second was not true, but injuries happen in almost every combat sport and martial art. You could be the most flexible and strongest person in your gym and still get hurt.

Injuries usually fall into two categories: contact and non-contact.

An example of a contact injury in BJJ would be getting taken down and landing on your shoulder.

An example of a non-contact injury would be twisting your ankle during a warm up.

As athletes, we do everything we can to try and avoid non-contact injuries and lessen the severity of the contact injuries. When an injury does happen it is devastating, physically and emotionally. A small injury that keeps us off the mats for a few weeks seems like an eternity. We are often in a rush to return to the mats and jump back into training.

But before you jump back into a competition class you need to test the waters. There are a few things you need to think through to increase your chances of a successful return. Consider taking these three steps:

Be Smart

Be smart about your training. It is so simple to say but difficult to follow. What is smart training? Smart training is training with the right intensity, training in the right positions, and training with the right partners.

The Right Level of Intensity

If you have been out for a while injured, then you are better off returning to the gym for a fundamental or beginner class, instead of a competition class. Once you feel your injured area is responding well to training, slowly start to increase your intensity.

The Right Moves and Positions

Often after an injury the type of BJJ game you play changes. For example, student who likes to play upside-down guard has now experienced a low back or neck injury. Playing upside-down guard is no longer a smart option.

Instead, this Jiu-Jitsu practitioner may choose to play a more closed guard game going forward. A second example is someone who likes to pass guard with a lot of cutting movements. After a knee tweak cutting movements might feel funny, so this student might consider a more over-under or stack passing game.

While it is easy to control your own BJJ game, it is difficult to control your training partners' games. Do not be afraid to tap fast and often. There is nothing wrong with tapping when you are in a compromised position. If you are coming back from a shoulder injury you want to tap early from a kimura. If a clever athlete who has a bad back gets stacked while someone is trying to pass guard, he or she will choose to tap or let the opponent pass without fighting it. This is the hardest part for most people because it means letting go of their ego.

The Right Training Partners

When you feel ready to test things out make sure you have a training partner you trust. Returning from an injury is not the time to roll with the new student you have never seen before. Pick a reliable and known partner who you like to train with. The perfect partner is one who lets you move at a good pace with control. Let them know are you are just coming back from an injury to make sure they are fully aware.

When you first get back on the mats you may feel great and want to get right back to where you left off. It is best to start off slowly and work your way back up. While you may feel great and have all your range of motion back, your injured area has not been challenged in any Jiu-Jitsu specific positions. A common example is returning to BJJ after a shoulder injury. Your shoulder may feel good, but as soon as you post for a hip-bump sweep your shoulder "feels odd." Until you test your injured area in BJJ-specific movements you may not know how it is going to feel, so be smart and be careful.

Your Self-Assessment

After you start to work your way back to full BJJ training it is important to take some time and think about how you got injured and what you can do differently this time around. Take some time and think about the following:

1. Did you over train?
2. Were you properly warmed up?
3. Did you get a good night sleep the day before you got injured?
4. Were you stressed out that day?
5. Did you tap when you should have (or not due to ego)?

It is vital to be completely honest with yourself to see if you can figure out if there were any external factors that contributed to your injury.

The proper training program

Every BJJ athlete needs to devote some time to corrective exercise and strength training. After an injury, take some time and assess your training program. Some injuries are a result of muscle imbalances, overuse or over-training. Does your program correct any imbalances you may have? Does your program incorporate corrective exercises and mobility work?

If you are missing any area from your program make sure you add it in. Most people design programs around their strengths when it is the weaknesses that need to be the focus. If you are strong, but have no mobility, then your next training phase should focus on mobility while maintaining strength. Conversely if you are mobile and flexible but not strong consider doing the reverse.

Why do so many students stop training? And how to stop it from being you

If I ask 100 random students "How long would you like to train Brazilian Jiu Jitsu?" the majority will answer "Forever."

If I ask 100 BJJ black belts, "What percentage of white and blue belt students on any given mat, will be training jiu-jitsu in 10 years?" they will answer somewhere between 2-6%.

From experience 10% of people quit because of the following reasons:

1. **Distance** - Life moves people around and sometimes away from the mat.
2. **Money** - Nothing in this world is free so when money is tight, Jiu-Jitsu classes sometimes take a hit.
3. **Family** - Family deserves more of your free time than anything else in the world.
4. **Work** - Sometimes work may get hectic which interferes with your training schedule.
5. **Injury** - All physical activities run the risk of injury and Brazilian Jiu-Jitsu is no exception.

I have found that 10% of BJJ student quit for the above reasons. However 90 - 100% uses them as excuses.

I believe that the number one reason students quit is expectations.

Your instructor, training partner, fellow teammates, and you all have expectations.

For instance, you may be a blue belt sparring with a white belt and find yourself in the middle of passing your partners guard. Within this scenario, not only is your instructor watching you spar, but all of the students at your academy are watching you as well. Your instructor may coach you through the guard-pass technique, but all the while, your partner has managed to sweep you. Often times, Brazilian Jiu-Jitsu students feel very emotionally attached to their belt rank.

Having a lower rank student sweep them in front of everyone at their gym can be an embarrassing experience. You may feel as though you let your coach down by not meeting their expectations of you and you may feel as though the students, who were watching you spar, now think less of your Jiu Jitsu technique. But the feeling of demoralization one may feel from a scenario such as this one, is completely subjective and only experienced as a result of someone feeling as though they have not met the expectations of others (Read: Their own ego).

In addition to having a white belt sweep you your coach may tell your training partner "nice sweep." Your own emotional attachment to perceived expectations (whether real or not), may cause you to overlook the bigger picture. Passing the guard is a very challenging task. Even if you get swept within your attempt to pass the guard, your attempt at passing the guard should still be counted as a step of progress in your BJJ journey. Unfortunately this accomplishment is often overshadowed by a person feeling as though they have not met expectations of the other people in the class, and overlooking your own progress because your coach complimented your training partner.

Imagine having experiences like these for 12 months. It is completely understandable that when you hurt your finger or are given more hours at your office job that would use these as excuses to say "I have to stop training for a month or two." Many students would feel embarrassed to tell their coach that they wanted to quit training because they felt as though they were not doing well.

However if the students were actually honest with their instructor and told them that they felt frustrated with their progress in training, then they would be surprised to learn of how accepting of a response they may receive. If you were to share how you were feeling with your instructor then they would probably respond "I remember feeling the same frustrations and you are not letting me down; BJJ works for us and against us."

And if you also mentioned how uncomfortable you feel knowing that your team mates on the mat feel that you are not deserving of your belt and how you yourself are starting to feel as if you are not deserving they may respond, "When on the Brazilian Jiu-Jitsu journey it is important that you do not compare yourself to anybody but yourself. There will always be someone younger, stronger, and faster than you. Although these characteristics are not prerequisites to learning jiu-jitsu, we cannot deny that being younger, stronger, and faster comes into play when technique is close to equal."

Next time you get swept, stuck on the bottom in side control, or even submitted; remember why you stepped on the mat in the first place. You were looking for something fun and challenging to do. BJJ is a place to escape the everyday noise of life while learning techniques and principles that you can apply to defend yourself in a street fight, competition or any life situation. We get all of these benefits and more when we train Brazilian Jiu-Jitsu. So do not tap to the expectations of others or your own, but instead, set a new expectation for yourself: Train BJJ for life.

Do not let the things that matter least, stand in the way of those which matter most.

Finally I will leave you with a quote from former UFC Fighter and BJJ black belt Kenny Florian

I wish people who stopped training in BJJ due to being discouraged realized how great they could become if they stick with it. #Persistence

- Kenny Florian

Other books by the same author

Beginning Judo: The Ultimate Guide to Starting Judo

Getting started in Judo can be daunting.

But training martial arts is one of the most beneficial things I've ever done, mentally and physically, but getting over the beginner's hump was where a chunk of those benefits come from.

Thankfully the Internet now allows us to learn more easily from those who came before us.

Here is what you will learn from reading Beginning Judo:

- What is Judo?
- What is the English translation or the meaning of the word Judo?
- What is the purpose in learning Judo?
- What are the main principles in learning Judo?
- Where did Judo come from?
- What is the difference between Judo and Traditional Jujitsu?
- What is the difference between Judo and Brazilian Jiu-Jitsu?
- Who created Judo?
- What are the different types of Judo throws?
- When did Judo become an Olympic sport?
- What are the Judo belt ranks?
- How to find a good Judo school?
- How to research your instructor?
- What does a typical Judo lesson consist of?

- Is Judo good for self defense?

- How long does it usually take to get a black belt in Judo?

- What does Randori (Sparring) look like?

- I'm concerned about getting hurt sparring. What should I do?

- And much more

Amazon US Link:

http://www.amazon.com/gp/product/B00VM9MC3Q

Amazon UK Link:

http://www.amazon.co.uk/gp/product/B00VM9MC3Q

MMA: Beginning MMA: The Ultimate Guide to MMA Training

As one of today's more popular fighting sports Mixed Martial Arts has captured the imagination of many aspiring fighting champions, as not only is it firmly rooted in many years of martial arts history and tradition - it evolved from both 1920's Brazilian Vale Tudo (no rules fighting) events and 1970's Japanese style shoot fighting. It also provides the perfect challenge for one who feels they have the necessary skills and abilities to fight at the highest level.

Here is a preview of what you will learn:

- What is MMA?
- Where to find an MMA Gym to train at
- How to research your instructor to check they are legitimate
- Find a Proper Training Environment
- What equipment you will need
- What you should wear to your first MMA class
- What to expect at your first MMA class
- What a typical MMA class looks like
- Beginner sparring tips
- Much, much more!

Amazon US Link:
http://www.amazon.com/gp/product/B00V3RKMWU

Amazon UK Link:
http://www.amazon.co.uk/gp/product/B00V3RKMWU

Printed in Great Britain
by Amazon